For Coleen.

Thanks for sticking with me through each one of life's revisions.

"Behold, days are coming," declares the Lord, "when I will make a new covenant with the house of Israel and with the house of Judah, not like the covenant which I made with their fathers in the day I took them by the hand to bring them out of the land of Egypt, My covenant which they broke, although I was a husband to them," declares the Lord. "But this is the covenant which I will make with the house of Israel after those days," declares the Lord, "I will put My law within them and on their heart I will write it; and I will be their God, and they shall be My people. They will not teach again, each man his neighbor and each man his brother, saying, 'Know the Lord,' for they will all know Me, from the least of them to the greatest of them," declares the Lord, "for I will forgive their iniquity, and their sin I will remember no more."

Jeremiah 31:31-34

Introduction:
A Case For ReVision

Today's college student may never know the dread of the red pen.

Modern word processing software allows teachers to make digital corrections in the margins of papers. They can click and drag to highlight areas that need attention. They can create links to a summary of their recommendations. These features have replaced the red pen.

Essential for English professors and feared by students, red marks in the body of a paper indicated that something was wrong. On several occasions, I received papers back with the notation "needs revision" next to paragraphs I'd already agonized over. My assignment, or my personal mission, in many classes was to write a paper that qualified for a good grade.

I understood the assignment, but the vision, the picture of what a good paper looked like, wasn't always easy to understand or accept. Frustration often embraced me when my vision of a good paper conflicted with my instructor's vision of a good paper. Buying into my instructor's vision helped me to accomplish my mission must faster than running with my own plan. There were several times when I attempted to write papers my own way, only to come back, after days of work, to my instructor's plan. I had to surrender to my instructor's red-inked suggestions.

> "Buying into my instructor's vision helped me to accomplish my mission must faster than running with my own plan."

Life can be similar to writing a paper.

I've come to understand my personal mission in life. My mission includes sharing messages of hope, healing, and inspiration. There was a time when I thought the perfect vision of that mission was only a life as a teacher. Then there was a revision. There was a time when I thought the perfect vision of that mission was only a life as a local church pastor. Then there was a revision. I'm learning that there may be multiple revisions necessary for me to fulfill my life's mission. A vision, the picture of what living out a mission looks like, may change several times, but for me, my mission stays the same.

Is it time for you to embrace the idea of a revision?

If you ask Webster, he'll say that a revision refers to changes for improvement, a new version of something, or to study information that was studied before. I won't argue with Webster, but I will suggest an addition to his menu of definitions. Here's what our working definition of revision will be for this book:

To imagine, dream, or plan again like it was the first time.

One of the most difficult things for me to do when working on a writing assignment was to make the decision to start over. I've been in situations where, after the instructor had read and made comments on a draft of my paper, it was clear that my best course of action was to begin again. My first attempt didn't hit the mark. A couple of tweaks here and there wouldn't be enough. I needed a complete overhaul. The most agonizing part was discarding something that I thought would work so well. Part of the revision process is accepting that what once felt great in one moment may be completely out of place in the next moment.

What if God is taking His own red pen and striking through our plans and even through some of His moves in the past? What if He is doing this not for us to ignore these past plans but to move us so we do not become shackled by them? What if He wants to us look at our lives and imagine, dream, or plan again like it was the first time? My hope, my wish, and my prayer for you is that you trust the process of revision so that your story can become even greater than what you originally thought was possible.

> "For I know the plans that I have for you," declares the LORD, "plans for welfare and not for calamity to give you a future and a hope."
>
> Jeremiah 29:11

Day 1

The Danger of Settling

When I first read the story of Helen Keller, I thought it was a fairy tale.

How does a girl ravaged by a sickness that leaves her deaf and blind go down in history as an international influencer? How does she become a political activist and a hero? How does she go on to lead a life of which most people only dream, despite her disabilities? The answer has two parts. The first part was her teacher Anne Sullivan, and the second part was her refusal to settle.

Anne Sullivan, who was also visually impaired, became Helen Keller's teacher. Sullivan knew the challenges of trying to navigate the world with physical limitations. Under her tutelage Keller flourished. Though learning proved difficult for Keller in the beginning, she refused to quit. What would have happened if eight-year-old Helen Keller gave up on the idea on trying to communicate? What if she had refused to follow the leadership of Anne Sullivan? What if she hadn't allowed herself to have another vision for her life, a vision that included making a difference in the world? If Helen Keller had settled, the world would never have known her name.

> "What if she hadn't allowed herself to have another vision for her life?"

The children of Israel desperately wanted to settle. Four hundred and thirty years of slavery had taken their drive, their hope, and their faith.

When the time was right, God sent Moses to lead them. I'm sure it took a bit of convincing for them to believe Moses. Armed with signs and wonders, Moses called for the children of Israel to vision again. He challenged them to believe that God had a place for them that was well beyond what they saw for themselves as slaves in Egypt.

On the march out of the Egypt, the plan hit a wrinkle. Pharaoh and the Egyptians weren't quite ready to accept life without Israel. They pursued Israel with reckless abandon. As soon as Israel heard the footsteps of the Egyptian army, they panicked. In that moment, they wanted to give up on their new vision. They wanted to chalk up the idea of the Promised Land to foolishness and succumb to their fears. Why not just go back to Egypt? They wondered why they even thought that anything else was possible. Maybe they should have just stuck with what they knew.

The great thing about this story is that their new vision for their lives was a God-given vision. God-given visions are the type of vision where the outcome is dependent on God but the responsibility to believe it will happen belongs to us. God wasn't about to let his people die at the hands of the Egyptians, even if Moses was the only one who believed. The temptation to settle stuck with Israel for years

"God-given visions are the type of vision where the outcome is dependent on God but the responsibility to believe it will happen belongs to us."

to come. Even after experiencing all the miracles of God, it was hard for them to believe that a different life was possible. Where in your life are you settling? Where are you in danger of sabotaging a new God-given vision for your life because you're afraid or because the journey is difficult? What might be possible if you refuse to settle?

"As Pharaoh drew near, the sons of Israel looked, and behold, the Egyptians were marching after them, and they became very frightened; so the sons of Israel cried out to the Lord. Then they said to Moses, "Is it because there were no graves in Egypt that you have taken us away to die in the wilderness? Why have you dealt with us in this way, bringing us out of Egypt? Is this not the word that we spoke to you in Egypt, saying, "Leave us alone that we may serve the Egyptians"? For it would have been better for us to serve the Egyptians than to die in the wilderness."

Exodus 14:10-12

Based on today's reading, what area(s) of your life might God be calling you to imagine, dream, or plan again?

Day 2

Pray For a New Vision

Michael Phelps won 28 Olympic medals in his career as a swimmer.

There every step of the way was his coach Bob Bowman. According to Coach Bowman, many successful athletes have one thing in common. They've pictured themselves winning long before they've actually won. Coach Bowman offered that months before actually winning in the pool, Phelps has already envisioned his success. Phelps had already lived out the sights, the sounds, and the experience of winning in his mind. Think about it. For every gold medal draped around his neck, Phelps had already experienced winning it. He probably never envisioned losing.

The unnamed servant of Elisha in 2 Kings only had a picture of Israel losing.

For years Israel had been ravaged by the Syrian army. The Syrian king struck fear in the heart of the king of Israel. Considered a world superpower at the time, Syria did not allow not much to get in its way. There were only two things that bothered the king of Syria. One was the idea that Elisha was not afraid of him, and the second was the fact that Elisha had insight into his private conversations. Seeing Elisha as a threat that needed to be exterminated, the king sent an army to capture or kill him. This great Army surrounded Dothan, the city where Elisha was staying. Can you imagine being a little boy or girl living in Dothan and waking up one day to the army surrounding the city? Elisha's servant had only known death and destruction at the hands of Syria. Maybe he had only been able to envision disappointment or oppression. Maybe he had conceded that his life would end at the hands of this vast army that had taken the lives of his friends and family members. Whatever was in his mind, he was not picturing a successful outcome. In desperation he cried out to Elisha, asking what they were going to do. The servant sounded exactly like I do when I feel surrounded and overwhelmed.

Elisha told the servant that he shouldn't worry because they themselves had a bigger army that the Syrians. Then, instead of going through an explanation, Elisha prayed that God would show his servant what Elisha had already seen. It was not that Elisha had already seen it with his own eyes but that his faith had helped him to see it in his mind. Elisha's prayer was for his servant to receive his own new vision.

What's amazing about Elisha's prayer is Elisha didn't ask to see for himself. He had already received the vision of deliverance by God's hand. If you had polled any of the residents of Dothan shortly after it was surrounded by the Syrians, I wonder how many of them would have believed that a rescue was possible.

"Elisha's prayer was for his servant to receive his own new vision."

As you start your journey of revision, maybe you feel the same way. The current vision that you have for your life, relationships, and ministry may have been damaged by disappointments and failures. You may have just accepted the idea that you're not worth saving or that nothing good happens to you. But here's the Biblical truth. God wants to give you a new vision, a vision of him surrounding you and you coming out a winner. If you ask him, he will help you believe it long before you experience it.

> "God wants to give you a new vision."

"Now when the attendant of the man of God had risen early and gone out, behold, an army with horses and chariots was circling the city. And his servant said to him, "Alas, my master! What shall we do?" So he answered, "Do not fear, for those who are with us are more than those who are with them." Then Elisha prayed and said, "O Lord, I pray, open his eyes that he may see." And the Lord opened the servant's eyes and he saw; and behold, the mountain was full of horses and chariots of fire all around Elisha."

2 Kings 6:15-17

Based on today's reading, what area(s) of your life might God be calling you to imagine, dream, or plan again?

Day 3

Write It Down and Wait

Dr. Gail Matthews from Dominican University in California conducted a study on goal achievement. The results of the study led Dr. Matthews to conclude that achieving your goals is influenced by three primary factors, accountability, commitment, and writing the goals down. Apparently having someone to hold you accountable for your goals, a strong sense of commitment to your goals, and plans for achieving them on paper makes a tremendous difference.

Did you write down your vision the first time?

If the answer is no, you're probably in good company. Take something simple like a trip to the grocery store. If you're anything like me, shopping without a list is a gamble. However, if I write my list on a piece of paper, there's a one hundred percent chance that I'll leave with everything I came for. The list gives me a picture of everything I need. It keeps me from getting in trouble with my wife for forgetting something important. The written list provides stability and focus amid the distractions of the store. Honestly, though, I'll admit that I don't always like taking the time to write things down. It seems like a nuisance until I actually need to remember what I need.

> "I'll admit that I don't always like taking the time to write things down."

Habakkuk was distracted.

The only thing that the prophet could see was what was going wrong. God's people had acted foolishly, and God had allowed the Babylonians to have temporary dominance over Judah. Habakkuk was frustrated that his people were suffering and it appeared that God was not responding. Habakkuk's plea was for God to pay attention to what was going on and do something about it. I'm sure we've all prayed a similar prayer. At the end of his prayer, however, Habakkuk came to his senses and realized that God was in control. In fact, Habakkuk knew that God would correct his lack of understanding. What was God's response to Habakkuk? God gave Habakkuk a vision and told him to write it down.

I believe that God still moves in this way today.

Problems.
Issues.
Insights.
Opportunities.

He gives a vision.

Once it was written down, it became more than the ramblings of an old prophet. I wonder how many times Habakkuk went back to his written vision on the days when he was struggling. How many times did he read those words to himself when the oppression from Babylon seemed unbearable? How many times did the words give him hope when he wanted to give up?

But writing down the vision didn't come easy. Some Bible translations say tables, and others say tablets. Either way, Habakkuk was probably writing on wood or stone. It took time to carve into stone or burn into wood what he needed to remember. A scroll would have been easier, but a stone lasts longer. Maybe God was letting the prophet know just how important this was. The time Habakkuk took to write or chisel would give him a deeper resonance with what God was eventually going to do.

Maybe it's hard for us to believe in the vision that God has given to us because we've been okay with keeping it locked in our heads. In a sense, if we write it, we release it. It will have to stand up to scrutiny or critique if it's on paper, but right now, it's safe in our heads. And what about the time it will take? Who wants to sit down with a blank computer screen, empty notebook, or note-taking app? If we keep our vision in our heads, there's less chance of being intimidated by it. We can wiggle around being accountable to it. Plus, if it doesn't work out, there will be no record of our failures. It's hard to resonate with something that we're not reminded about.

Or maybe writing it down is one of the biggest faith steps that we can take. God told Habakkuk to write it down and

> "Maybe writing it down is one of the biggest faith steps that we can take."

wait for it because it was coming. I don't think that was a passive waiting. I think God was telling Habakkuk to write it down and wait in anticipation for the outcome. While he waited, he would have a stone or wood reminder to refresh his memory. No one is calling you to break out the chisel or the wood-burning pen, but you are called to get the vision out of your head and written down in a place you can remember.

"Then the Lord answered me and said, "Record the vision and inscribe it on tablets, That the one who reads it may run. "For the vision is yet for the appointed time; It hastens toward the goal and it will not fail. Though it tarries, wait for it; For it will certainly come, it will not delay."
Habakkuk 2:2-3

Reflections:

Based on today's reading, what area(s) of your life might God be calling you to imagine, dream, or plan again?

Day 4

Divorce the "How"

The Library of Congress suggests that it may be difficult to nail down exactly who built the first car, but they vote for Karl Benz. The Smithsonian Institute lumps Benz's name in with host of other European inventors. For centuries to come, we may continue to debate who actually came up with and implemented the idea first. We could even argue about whose methods were the best. The truth is that how they did it is not as important as what they did.

Henry Ford is known for having pioneered the assembly line, and it is believed that he once said, "If I had asked people what they wanted, they would have said faster horses." Many people would not have even been able to envision such progress as an automobile. They already had horses. Why not focus on how to make them go faster?

The "what" was simple. Get people from one place to another as fast as possible. This was the mission. This was the focus. For Karl Benz, Henry Ford, and everyone else who contributed to the automobile revolution, the "how" was up for debate. And it still is. The world has since been exposed to steam-powered, gas-powered, and electric cars, as a reminder that if you keep the "what" in review, the "how" is always subject to interpretation.

I once pastored a small congregation of about 20 people. The church building was roughly the size of a small house. The sanctuary could hold around 100 people. The fellowship with tables and chairs comfortably sat 40. The foundation was shifting, the floors were creaky, the walls were moldy, and the electricity was spotty. We faithfully prayed weekly for God to send us a miracle. Many in the congregation were on a fixed income and often faced financial difficulty.

One of the members who had grown up in the church said that he didn't bring his kids because the facility didn't meet their needs. I wonder how many visitors over the years felt the same way.

While reviewing the history of the church, I fear that it may have missed its miracle because it was married to the how instead of the what. The church sat across the street from a major hospital. Several years back, the hospital offered to buy the property from the church for close to $400,000. They wanted to convert the space into additional parking. The church refused to sell. They couldn't see themselves letting go of the history, the memories, or their vision of what was supposed to happen in the neighborhood. We begged God for a miracle, but maybe we missed it because we didn't like how He sent it.

What if the church had accepted the offer? What if they had been able to build a better facility? What if they had addressed the needs in the community by letting go of good memories in the past and looking forward to greater memories in the future? God consistently promises to take care of his children. Our frustration develops when we want to

"God consistently promises to take care of his children."

prescribe the "how." God doesn't often give a clear "how," but he does always give a clear "what."

When you look at your life, your family, your faith community, your business, and your team, what are you being called to do? Where have you faced challenges because you thought that your "how" was the only way that things should work? Revision requires us to never forget the "what" and to allow God to blow our minds with the myriad of "hows" he has at his disposal.

"Go therefore and make disciples of all the nations, baptizing them in the name of the Father and the Son and the Holy Spirit, teaching them to observe all that I commanded you; and lo, I am with you always, even to the end of the age."

Matthew 28:19-20

Reflections:

Based on today's reading, what area(s) of your life might God be calling you to imagine, dream, or plan again?

Day 5

Mission (Purpose) Reminded

I finally got around to reading the Chick-Fil-A mission statement.

If you've eaten at a Chick-Fil-A you'll probably agree that they are living out their mission. When you step to the counter, you are always greeted with a "How may I serve you?" When you thank them, "My pleasure" is their response. Everything about the experience exudes warmth and friendliness.

When you read their mission statement, it just make sense. They don't call it a mission statement. For Chick-Fil-A it's a purpose statement. Feel free to use the terms interchangeably.

> "To glorify God by being a faithful steward of all that is entrusted to us."

The mission of an organization is the reason why it exists. As listed on their website, their purpose statement reads: To glorify God by being a faithful steward of all that is entrusted to us and to have a positive influence on all who come into contact with Chick-Fil-A.

Chick-Fil-A serves chicken. Most people who stop by are purchasing some chicken-related product. As a company, however, serving chicken is not their purpose. Their purpose is to positively influence you, no matter what you purchase. Saying hello, wiping off tables, and having someone stand outside and hand you your food so you don't have to reach far into the drive-through window are all how they do it.

I wonder how long it takes new employees to catch on that their job is about more than chicken sandwiches. Chick-fil-A is selling positive influence, and people continue to buy. Chick-fil-A made $5.8 billion in 2014 and continues to be one of the top ten fast food chains in the US. That's quite a bit of chicken, but more than that, it's more than a handful of "How many I serve yous," "Thank yous," and "My pleasures" that keep people coming back for the chicken.

Jerusalem appeared to have abandoned its mission.

Geographically it was located in an elevated place. You couldn't miss it if you were passing by. In the Old Testament, King David had conquered Jerusalem and built it into a great city. Eventually the Ark of the Covenant, which was connected to the presence of God, was brought to Jerusalem. Solomon's temple was an architectural wonder and people traveled from miles around to experience it. More than a conquest of war and an attraction, Jerusalem was set up by God to be a place where outsiders encountering His people would learn about Him. Jerusalem's mission was to share the message of God, who had done all these amazing things.

> "Jerusalem was set up by God to be a place where outsiders encountering His people would learn about Him."

Roughly translated to mean "city of peace," Jerusalem had since become full of tension. By the time Jesus arrived on the scene, the city has lost some of its luster. It was still a point of attraction geographically, but it was not capitalizing on its location to be a place of witness. No wonder Jesus challenged the inhabitants of Jerusalem in his Sermon on the Mount. His attempt was to remind them of their mission. He wanted to refresh their thinking about their purpose. It wasn't just to exist comfortably, but to recount their blessings from God to others. They were placed by God to witness to the nations around them. Instead of doing this, the culture had a way of merely enjoying its special distinction.

> "He wanted to refresh their thinking about their purpose."

Jesus was seeking a revision for Jerusalem. Part of Jesus' effort was to make his people more mission-minded, but they were having none of that. They had made their mission themselves. Jesus cried his eyes out over the fact that Jerusalem rejected him.

When organizations have an internal focus, they lose the ability to impact those they once said they cared about. What would the Chick-fil-A experience be like if the employees only cared about serving themselves? You probably wouldn't be greeted with a smile. It wouldn't be their pleasure to serve you. They wouldn't care how the place looked or whether they made a good impression on you. If it was all about them, they wouldn't care about you.

Your revision may mean considering your original mission or purpose and moving back to center. How close to your mission or how far from it are you and your organization now? How does being off-mission impact those you are called to serve?

"You are the salt of the earth; but if the salt has become tasteless, how can it be made salty again? It is no longer good for anything, except to be thrown out and trampled under foot by men. You are the light of the world. A city set on a hill cannot be hidden; nor does anyone light a lamp and put it under a basket, but on the lampstand, and it gives light to all who are in the house. Let your light shine before men in such a way that they may see your good works, and glorify your Father who is in heaven."

Matthew 5:13-16

Reflections:

Based on today's reading, what area(s) of your life might God be calling you to imagine, dream, or plan again?

Day 6

Move Beyond Yesterday

I was rummaging through and old supply closet and found a box of floppy disks. If you have no idea what I'm talking about, just Google "save icon." A floppy disk used to be the technological wonder of computer storage. Created in the 1960s, the first floppy disk was about eight square inches of flat vinyl, and its material gave it a floppy quality. The storage capacity was a whopping 256k or .256 megabytes. As time moved on, the actual size of the disk kept getting smaller while the storage capacity kept getting better. I grew up in the time of the 3.5-inch disk that held 1.4 megabyte of information. It was a box of these disks that I had stumbled upon.

I had a quick flashback to writing papers and storing them on floppy disks. The technology was convenient at the time and made the transfer of information easier. Today, using floppy disks would be cumbersome. My smartphone storage capacity is 16 gigabytes. It would take roughly 11,000 floppy disks to equal the storage capacity of the one smartphone. Can you imagine trying to work on a project today with your only option for storage being floppy disks? The children of Israel had essentially built a shrine to a floppy disk.

"The children of Israel had essentially built a shrine to a floppy disk."

In the Old Testament book Numbers, God was dealing with the complaints of his

32

people. They complained often! While moving through the land of Edom, they were rehearsing their same old complaint. Even after all the miracles they had seen, they still worried about food and water. Complaints drowned out the possibility of remembering what they should have been grateful for. In an instant, God temporarily removed his protective covering from the children of Israel. Snakes moved in and started biting with reckless abandon. Moses prayed, and God provided a remedy. He told Moses to make a snake similar to the ones that were biting the people and put it up on a pole, and anyone who looked at the snake on the pole would survive any snakebite.

A miracle.
Amazing.
A must-tell story for future generations.
But years later they just couldn't let the snake go.

By the time Hezekiah became king and began to reign in Jerusalem, the snake on a pole had become more than just a legend. It had become an idol. As the leader, Hezekiah decided to tear down and break up what had once been the symbol of one of God's miracles in the wilderness. For years his people had worshiped the reminder of what God had done. They burned incense to it. They offered prayers to it. They even gave it a name, Nehushtan. They were celebrating the tool of deliverance instead of the deliverer himself. Hezekiah recognized that if his people had any chance of moving forward, it was dependent upon getting rid of the snake.

I wonder how that conversation went with his leaders. I wonder how much pushback he got from his elders. Did they look on in horror as Hezekiah explained his plan? Did they embrace the vision of what was possible, or did they call for a meeting to have Hezekiah removed? Hezekiah stands as a reminder that part of a leader's responsibility includes tipping our hat at what once was a great thing before we tear it down so that something greater can take its place.

> "Now it came about in the third year of Hoshea, the son of Elah king of Israel, that Hezekiah the son of Ahaz king of Judah became king. He was twenty-five years old when he became king, and he reigned twenty-nine years in Jerusalem; and his mother's name was Abi the daughter of Zechariah. He did right in the sight of the Lord, according to all that his father David had done. He removed the high places and broke down the sacred pillars and cut down the Asherah. He also broke in pieces the bronze serpent that Moses had made, for until those days the sons of Israel burned incense to it; and it was called Nehushtan."
>
> 2 Kings 18:1-4

Reflections:

Based on today's reading, what area(s) of your life might God be calling you to imagine, dream, or plan again?

Day 7

Beware of Chasing Ghosts

One of the greatest things that former NBA basketball player Kobe Bryant did was choosing to pattern his style of play after NBA legend Michael Jordan. This also might have been one of the worst decisions he ever made. When Jordan retired from basketball, Bryant spent the rest of his career chasing Jordan's ghost.

He could never be Michael Jordan. Kobe lost in the NBA finals. Jordan never lost in the finals. Kobe won five championships, and Jordan won six. Kobe won the most valuable player award once. Jordan won five times. The list goes on and on.

Kobe made his mark in the NBA, and his efforts have forever been etched in NBA history. But in the back of sports aficionados' minds, the thought that Kobe never eclipsed Jordan's accomplishments still looms. For some, Kobe never had a chance. How could he? He wasn't Michael Jordan.

At one point in my ministry, I was pastoring three small congregations. In one of these churches, the pictures of the former pastors donned the hallway. They were a focal point in the lobby. One portrait was of the man who had founded the church in the 1800s. One picture was of a pastor known for his dynamic preaching. Another was of a pastor who had led the church through a major renovation project. They had even carved his name in a brick outside the church.

Each time I stepped into the church, I had a visual reminder of what I wasn't. For the first year, I was unsettled. How could I ever do anything in a place where so many greats had mounted the pulpit before me? My vision of who I was called to impact was almost derailed because I was stuck trying to chase ghosts.

I wonder if Joshua ever felt like he was chasing a ghost. The greatest leader in the history of Israel had left him in charge. Moses had received a great upbringing. He had experienced the finer things in life along with military training. Balanced, diplomatic, and strong-willed, Moses was a great leader. Joshua wasn't Moses. He didn't have the same training, background, or education. Joshua could never be Moses. He could only be Joshua.

Joshua's vision was to get his people to the Promised Land. When you read the story, it's clear that Joshua didn't do things the way that Moses did. It's also clear that the children of Israel made it to the Promised Land under Joshua's leadership. If Joshua had spent his life chasing the ghost of Moses, he would have never been able to follow the vision that God gave him. We are not called to be as good as those who have come before us. We are called to pursue our God-given vision and be the leaders that God has called us to be.

"We are not called to be as good as those who have come before us. We are called to pursue our God-given vision and be the leaders that God has called us to be."

"So the sons of Israel wept for Moses in the plains of Moab thirty days; then the days of weeping and mourning for Moses came to an end. Now Joshua the son of Nun was filled with the spirit of wisdom, for Moses had laid his hands on him; and the sons of Israel listened to him and did as the Lord had commanded Moses. Since that time no prophet has risen in Israel like Moses, whom the Lord knew face to face, for all the signs and wonders which the Lord sent him to perform in the land of Egypt against Pharaoh, all his servants, and all his land, and for all the mighty power and for all the great terror which Moses performed in the sight of all Israel."

Deuteronomy 34:8-12

Reflections:

Based on today's reading, what area(s) of your life might God be calling you to imagine, dream, or plan again?

Day 8

Adjusting to the Interruption

When I fly I like to pick my seat.

I have a routine for air travel, and carefully picking my seat is part of that routine. I don't mind exit rows, but window seats are a must. I also try to avoid the back of the plane at all costs. I like to control what I can control. So staring down at my boarding pass after checking in and seeing the instructions to report to the counter for a seat assignment didn't exactly bring me comfort. But what choice did I have? Someone else made the travel arrangements for me. My assignment was to show up at the gate.

After inching at a turtle's pace through security I found my way to my gate and eventually handed my temporary boarding pass to the agent. My freshly-printed ticket awaited me on the desk. I peered down at the seat assignment, 23D. It sounded close to the front or the middle at least. I didn't give much thought to the fact that I was flying on a small plane. Boarding the plane, I counted the aisles while looking for my seat. 16, 17, 18, 19 ... there it was, 23D, the last seat. There was no recline option, and I was near the bathroom. I felt a complaint bubbling up on the inside. I pushed the complaint away and made a new plan to make the most of this trip. Despite my discomfort, I was prepared to make it work.

Before I could get settled in, the flight attendant approached me. He mentioned something about weight balance and moving me to first class. I excitedly waited for him to escort me there. Instead he pointed and told me to make my way to the front of the plane. I was excited about the opportunity but not excited about carrying my belonging the length of the plane again. For a few fleeting moments, the effort of relocating made me think that 23D wouldn't have been too bad. At least I was settled. My first class seat shattered these notions. The better view, leg room, and wider, more comfortable seat were worth the relocation.

I wonder what Abraham's plans were and which direction he planned to go.

At the time of his father Terah's death, Abraham's name was Abram, which meant exalted father. We have no evidence of Abram receiving a large inheritance. His genealogy doesn't offer many notable names. It doesn't appear that he had much to fall back on. Maybe Abram planned to go back to the land of Ur. Maybe his vision was to live out his days in peace while mourning the death of his father. As Abram began to settle with his plan, God showed up with a command.

"Get up and go."

God presented Abram with an edited vision for his life. Abram would not live out his days among his relatives. He would go on one of the greatest journeys on Biblical record. His name would be changed to Abraham, which meant "father of many." Along the way, he would also acquire wealth and a small army. In a few words, God gave Abraham a vision of a first-class life. He just didn't tell him how it would happen.

What if Abraham had said no?

What if he had decided the journey was too much or that God was taking too long to fulfill his promises? What if he had been content with living out his days with his relatives instead of going on this life-altering journey? What if he had refused to accept the God-given vision for his life?

> "What if he had refused to accept the God-given vision for his life?"

I think about how my flight would have been if I'd decided that the walk to first class was too much of an effort. How much regret would I have felt if I'd let fear of the stares of the other passengers keep me in my seat?

How much would I have kicked myself for choosing to stay in a place of discomfort when there was a better option available? I'm glad I chose to get up and go.

"Now the Lord said to Abram, 'Go forth from your country, and from your relatives, and from your father's house, to the land which I will show you; and I will make you a great nation, and I will bless you, and make your name great; and so you shall be a blessing; and I will bless those who bless you, and the one who curses you I will curse. and in you all the families of the earth will be blessed.' So Abram went forth as the Lord had spoken to him; and Lot went with him. Now Abram was seventy-five years old when he departed from Haran. Abram took Sarai his wife and Lot his nephew, and all their possessions which they had accumulated, and the persons which they had acquired in Haran, and they set out for the land of Canaan; thus they came to the land of Canaan. Abram passed through the land as far as the site of Shechem, to the oak of Moreh. Now the Canaanite *was* then in the land. The Lord appeared to Abram and said, 'To your descendants I will give this land.' So he built an altar there to the Lord who had appeared to him."

Genesis 12:1-7

Reflections:

Based on today's reading, what area(s) of your life might God be calling you to imagine, dream, or plan again?

Day 9

Stop Dumbing it Down

Phillippe Petit is a French high wire artist.

At 16, Petit took a walk on a high wire and was never the same. At 18, he heard about the plans to build the Twin Towers in New York, and he set his sights on walking a rope between those towers. It was a vision that took six years to realize. Part of the reason that it took so long was because the towers weren't built yet. Talk about preparing for something you haven't seen!

While Petit waited he worked to ready himself.

In 1971 he walked between to the towers of the Notre Dame Cathedral in Paris. In 1973 he walked between the pylons of the Sydney Harbor Bridge in Australia. These were nothing to shake a stick at, but they weren't the Twin Towers.

I wonder if Petit ever wanted to give up. I wonder if he had second thoughts about trying to get his equipment to the tops of the towers. I wonder if he almost gave up when there was a problem with his method of raising his wire and his team had to spend hours pulling a 450-pound cable to the top of one of the towers. I wonder if he thought about tightrope walking between two shorter buildings instead. I wonder if he had a momentary impulse to say his previous feats were good enough.

> "I wonder if Petit ever wanted to give up."

Elisha was both a prophet and a counselor to kings. Near the end of his life, Elisha advised King Jehoash of Israel, whose land was under siege by the Syrians. Jehoash was overcome with fear of what might happen to the armies of Israel. The Syrians had slapped around Israel's army before, and Jehoash feared that this would be the end of them.

Elisha provided a faith object lesson for the distraught king. He first told him to take up a bow and shoot an arrow in the direction of the Syrians. This symbolized that Israel was calling for a fight. Then Elisha asked Jehoash to grab more arrows and strike the ground with them. This would symbolize the amount of damage Israel would do to the Syrians. Jehoash struck the ground three times. Elisha was frustrated. He thought the king would have kept going. Maybe Jehoash couldn't envision a complete annihilation of the Syrians by the Israelites. Maybe it was difficult because he had never imagined the possibility before. Maybe his fear of them was so great that he didn't see any way out. Jehoash dumbed down the vision of what was possible, and as a result he lost the opportunity to get rid of the Syrians completely.

> "Jehoash dumbed down the vision of what was possible."

If the message comes to strike the ground, keep striking until you're told to stop. If the message is to keep climbing, don't let your fear of the size of the tower keep you on the ground. If God gives you the vision for something great, don't dumb it down to something you feel comfortable accomplishing on your own.

Then he said, "Take the arrows," and he took them. And he said to the king of Israel, "Strike the ground," and he struck it three times and stopped. So the man of God was angry with him and said, "You should have struck five or six times, then you would have struck Aram until you would have destroyed it. But now you shall strike Aram only three times."

2 Kings 13:18-19

Reflections:

Based on today's reading, what area(s) of your life might God be calling you to imagine, dream, or plan again?

Day 10

You Need Less Than You Think

There's something about underdog stories that make us cheer.

History is full of stories of underdogs becoming victorious. This was certainly the case for the English troops in one of the battles between England and France during the Hundred Years' War.

The Hundred Years' War was a conflict about the right to rule, succession, and territories.

One of the pivotal battles in the war was the Battle of Agincourt. On October 25, 1845, King Henry V led roughly 9,000 English troops into battle against the over 35,000 that made up the French deployment. The French anticipated that the battle would be an easy win. Some historians even suggest that the French didn't see a need to deploy their best soldiers. When the battle was over, the English had done the unthinkable. Though severely outnumbered, they wreaked havoc on the French army and won the battle.

Gideon was a clear Biblical underdog.

Gideon never really saw himself as much. In society's eyes, Gideon's family wasn't much, and he wasn't much in comparison with the rest of his family. Many would consider this a double disqualification from importance. While hiding from the Midianites who had oppressed his people, Gideon received a message from God. Gideon would lead the children of Israel to victory. I'm sure Gideon thought the idea was crazy, having never imagined that his life would be different. Maybe he had the horrifying recurring dream of living out his days hiding from the Midianites. The idea of being a champion had never crossed his mind.

Gideon needed to dream again.

God was about to give Gideon a new vision. Through a series of signs, Gideon was finally convinced that God was serious about this mission. As Gideon prepared to train with 32,000 men, he might have had a shot of confidence, a confidence that was probably shaken when God reduced the numbers. His army of 32,000 was trimmed to 300. Gideon was stunned, but God was clear. If you have too many men, people may get the wrong idea about where your victory really came from. God gave Gideon less than Gideon thought he needed so that he would have no choice but to depend on God.

> "Through a series of signs, Gideon was finally convinced that God was serious about this mission."

Gideon's story challenges us to think more of ourselves, not necessarily that we are better than we think we are but that there is so much more that God wants to accomplish in us. Regardless of familial upbringing or social status, He has a greater vision for what He wants us to accomplish. We should also be careful of thinking that we need everything in place before we move forward. There are times for cosigners, supports, and cheerleaders for our vision. There are also times when God calls us to move forward with just a few. God has an amazing track record of accomplishing more with less.

"The Lord said to Gideon, "The people who are with you are too many for Me to give Midian into their hands, for Israel would become boastful, saying, 'My own power has delivered me.' Now therefore come, proclaim in the hearing of the people, saying, 'Whoever is afraid and trembling, let him return and depart from Mount Gilead.'" So 22,000 people returned, but 10,000 remained. Then the Lord said to Gideon, "The people are still too many; bring them down to the water and I will test them for you there. Therefore it shall be that he of whom I say to you, 'This one shall go with you,' he shall go with you; but everyone of whom I say to you, 'This one shall not go with you,' he shall not go." So he brought the people down to the water. And the Lord said to Gideon, "You shall separate everyone who laps the water with his tongue as a dog laps, as well as everyone who kneels to drink." Now the number of those who lapped, putting their hand to their mouth, was 300 men; but all the rest of the people kneeled to drink water. The Lord said to Gideon, "I will deliver you with the 300 men who lapped and will give the Midianites into your hands; so let all the other people go, each man to his home."

Judges 7:2-7

Reflections:

Based on today's reading, what area(s) of your life might God be calling you to imagine, dream, or plan again?

Day 11

It Will Probably Look Different

Long before the days of saving things in the "cloud," saving your research paper writing was a bit of a gamble.

In a moment's notice, all of your hard work could do up in digital smoke. Your hard drive could crash or the files on your portable storage device could be deleted accidentally. Or even worse, you could have forgotten to save your work before closing the word processing application. Autosave wasn't always a thing.

I been there before. I've poured out my heart and soul into a paper only to lose it. The painstaking process of writing it again tortured me. No matter how much I tried, I could never get the recreated paper to feel the same way as the one I'd lost. Even if I received high marks on the paper, I still longed for my previous work.

Imagine having the experience of walking through Solomon's temple. The majesty, the grandeur, and the opulence made an amazing sight to behold. Solomon spared no expense in building a temple to God. People traveled from miles around to catch a glimpse of this architectural marvel. Eventually, however, the temple was destroyed, and God's people were taken captive. A prophecy declared that Cyrus would free God's people and finance the rebuilding of the temple.

The prophet Ezra notes the experience. It was a mixed bag. There were some who were excited to again have a central place for worship. They shouted for joy. Others, however, met the new temple with tears. Tears were their only response. What they were experiencing couldn't hold a candle to the old temple. To them, this seemed like a shoddy substitute.

The shouts of joy were mixed with the cries of despair, and you could hardly tell the two apart.

The prophet Haggai would later offer some hope. Haggai 2:9 says that though the second temple could not match the first in outward appearance, it would surpass the first temple in importance. How would this be possible? Jesus himself would arrive on the scene. It would be at this temple that he would be dedicated as a baby, challenge the leaders as a child, and teach the people as an adult. No amount of gold, silver, or incense could match God living among his people in the flesh.

What God is calling you to do next might not have the same outward flare and beauty as something that he previously called you to do. In fact, we often get bogged down by over-celebrating our glory days. What if a greater demonstration of God's glory is possible in our lives only if we refuse to be limited by the ways that he has demonstrated his glory in the past? Your revision might not look greater than what came before, but it might have greater impact when you start to live it out.

"Yet many of the priests and Levites and heads of fathers' households, the old men who had seen the first temple, wept with a loud voice when the foundation of this house was laid before their eyes, while many shouted aloud for joy, so that the people could not distinguish the sound of the shout of joy from the sound of the weeping of the people, for the people shouted with a loud shout, and the sound was heard far away."

Ezra 3:12-13

Reflections:

Based on today's reading, what area(s) of your life might God be calling you to imagine, dream, or plan again?

Day 12

God-Given Vision Requires God-Given Instructions

Have you ever put together furniture that arrived in a box?

Like me, you might just be a sucker for the display model. In the store you see a bookshelf, desk, or dresser that you think would be perfect for your home. Grabbing a cart, you take a box off the shelf below it and head home with the vision of a new piece of furniture in your mind. At home you open the box and remove the contents. The instructions fall out of the box, and you lay them to the side. You have the vision of what you experienced in the store, you have the picture on the box, and you have the materials. What else do you need?

> "Even though I know how it will turn out, I have still made several attempts to assemble furniture without the instructions."

Even though I know how it will turn out, I have still made several attempts to assemble furniture without the instructions. Every time something goes wrong. I have too many screws left. Something doesn't fit right. The final product is too shaky to use. My failed attempt forces me to disassemble what I have done and pick up the instructions I have laid to the side. Had I just used them in the first place, I could have avoided the headache.

God gave Abram a revision for his life.

After the death of Abram's father, God called him to leave his family and go to an unknown place. God gave Abram the promise that one day he would be the father of many. That's a crazy thing to say to an old man married to a woman who is unable to have kids, but Abram believed God, went on the journey, and was blessed tremendously by God. But years passed since the promise was given, and Abram still didn't have children, so his wife Sarai made a suggestion. Sarai urged Abram to take her maid Hagar and have a child with her. Sarai planned to take the child of Abram and Hagar as her own. Abram agreed and Hagar got pregnant, but this caused a rift between Hagar and Sarai.

Eventually Hagar and her son Ishmael were kicked out of Abram's house, and Ishmael grew up as a fatherless child, all because Abram agreed to try to work out God's vision without God's instructions. Can you relate? Has God ever given you a clear picture of what you were supposed to do, but because you were impatient, you made decisions that weren't Spirit-led? In your excitement to get something done, have you ever opened a door that you knew wasn't part of God's plan? Have you ever had to deal with the consequences of moving too far and too fast? God will speak to you again. He will give you insight. He has a vision for you. This time, be patient and wait for clear instructions before you end up making a big mess of things.

> "Has God ever given you a clear picture of what you were supposed to do, but because you were impatient, you made decisions that weren't Spirit-led?"

"Now Sarai, Abram's wife had borne him no children, and she had an Egyptian maid whose name was Hagar. So Sarai said to Abram, "Now behold, the Lord has prevented me from bearing children. Please go in to my maid; perhaps I will obtain children through her." And Abram listened to the voice of Sarai. After Abram had lived ten years in the land of Canaan, Abram's wife Sarai took Hagar the Egyptian, her maid, and gave her to her husband Abram as his wife. He went in to Hagar, and she conceived; and when she saw that she had conceived, her mistress was despised in her sight. And Sarai said to Abram, "May the wrong done me be upon you. I gave my maid into your arms, but when she saw that she had conceived, I was despised in her sight. May the Lord judge between you and me." But Abram said to Sarai, "Behold, your maid is in your power; do to her what is good in your sight." So Sarai treated her harshly, and she fled from her presence."

Genesis 16:1-6

Reflections:

Based on today's reading, what area(s) of your life might God be calling you to imagine, dream, or plan again?

Day 13

Risks Aren't Optional

I can't swim.

After revealing this to my church, I was met at the door by someone who serves as a swimming coach. He gave me a flyer with his number and told me to call him about lessons. The thought of getting into the swimming pool doesn't exactly frighten me, but it does make me feel uncomfortable. I was presented with an incredible opportunity to learn how to swim from a well-qualified instructor, but I'm just sitting on it because of the risk.

The risk is looking foolish. The risk is being watched. The risk is some young kid pointing out the old guy who can't swim. All these are real possibilities, and if I want to learn how to swim, I can't avoid them. Now my mission is to muster up enough courage to begin taking lessons while I still have the opportunity.

> "The risk is looking foolish. The risk is being watched."

Jesus tells a story about a man who, while preparing to go on a trip, gave his servants money. Each of them was given a certain amount according to what they were able to handle. The term "talents" was used to refer to the weight of the money they received. The first servant was given five talents, the second servant was given two talents, and the third servant was given one talent.

When the master returned, the first two servants had doubled what was given to them. The third servant had hid the money in the ground. During this time, hiding money in the ground for safekeeping was a good idea, but the master in the story wasn't interested in his servant playing it safe. He wanted to his servant to take a risk. It was possible that, by taking risk and investing or trading, he could have lost everything, and this risk had scared the servant into his choice to bury it. His master was furious. He would have preferred for his servant to take a chance and lose it all instead of playing it safe.

I see much of this third servant in myself. Trips to the beach are not quite as fun for me. Water parks aren't my cup of tea. This is all because I haven't taken the risk to learn how to swim. Who knows, there could be an incredible swimmer locked inside me, but my fear of risk is keeping him in bondage. I do have visions of teaching my daughters how to swim, but that vision will only become a reality on the other side of risk.

In what ways are you playing it safe when it comes to your God-given vision? What are a few of the things that would be possible if you faced your fears and took a chance to walk in the direction that God is calling you?

> "And the one also who had received the one talent came up and said, "Master, I knew you to be a hard man, reaping where you did not sow and gathering where you scattered no seed. And I was afraid, and went away and hid your talent in the ground. See, you have what is yours."
> Matthew 25:24-25

Reflections:

Based on today's reading, what area(s) of your life might God be calling you to imagine, dream, or plan again?

Day 14

Guarding The Vision

Ry Stephen is kicking himself for not guarding his recipes better.

In 2015, Stephen, who owns Mr. Holmes Bakehouse in San Francisco, was the victim of a break-in. Instead of taking money, equipment, or computers, the culprit stole over 200 recipes. The most famous of these is Stephen's recipe for the cruffin, a marriage between a croissant and a muffin that takes three days to make. The theft may have been avoided had the security system that was recently installed in the store been up and running. It wasn't. Many news outlets reported that the recipe for the cruffin didn't include many of the essential details, so it can't be used to make the legendary cruffin, but what if it did? What if imitation cruffins started popping up all over the place because of a lack of security?

Have you ever woken up from a dream and just couldn't keep it to yourself? Then, in the middle of explaining it to someone else, you realized that you were starting to sound crazy to them. Part of you wished that you had just kept the whole thing to yourself. This was exactly what happened to Joseph. Joseph was the favorite son. You can imagine all the relational dynamics at play, because you probably have favorites in your family too.

Joseph had two dreams. Both the dreams appeared to describe Joseph rising to prominence while his family bowed before him. If your brother or sister or child explained something similar, how would you feel? The dream disturbed the entire family. Joseph's brothers were jealous, and his father challenged him but kept the idea in the back of his mind. Ultimately, Joseph was sold into slavery, because his brother couldn't keep in the family someone who thought he would one day be served by them. I wonder how many times on the trip to Egypt Joseph kicked himself for opening his mouth. We all know how the story worked out, but what we will never know is how God would have worked it out had Joseph been quiet about it.

"The dream disturbed the entire family."

When was the last time someone tried to crush your vision? When was the last time you opened up to someone about what God put in your heart and they thought you were crazy? What has your experience been with someone trying to undercut your vision because it may place you a little higher than them? The next time God gives you a vision, be very careful who you share it with. Guard it at all costs. Don't give people the opportunity to steal the passion and desire that you have for it. When the time is right, God will guide you to share your vision with those around it you.

"Then Joseph had a dream, and when he told it to his brothers, they hated him even more. He said to them, "Please listen to this dream which I have had; for behold, we were binding sheaves in the field, and lo, my sheaf rose up and also stood erect; and behold, your sheaves gathered around and bowed down to my sheaf." Then his brothers said to him, "Are you actually going to reign over us? Or are you really going to rule over us?" So they hated him even more for his dreams and for his words. Now he had still another dream, and related it to his brothers, and said, "Lo, I have had still another dream; and behold, the sun and the moon and eleven stars were bowing down to me." He related it to his father and to his brothers; and his father rebuked him and said to him, "What is this dream that you have had? Shall I and your mother and your brothers actually come to bow ourselves down before you to the ground?" His brothers were jealous of him, but his father kept the saying in mind."

Genesis 37:5-11

Reflections:

Based on today's reading, what area(s) of your life might God be calling you to imagine, dream, or plan again?

Day 15

You Thought It Was Going To Be Easy?

I was excited when I arrived on campus to start seminary studies.

It had only been a year since I had taken a good job with a nonprofit in the DC area. I worked in donor relations, and my job was to maintain a program that kept donors up to date with the stories of the organization's work in the field. It was good work and I had some good colleagues, but it just wasn't the job for me. It took some time, but I was finally willing to accept a new direction, so my family packed up and moved back to Berrien Springs, Michigan.

How hard could seminary really be, I thought to myself. I was a pretty good Bible student, I had a basic grasp of theology, and I could put presentations together with ease. To top it all off, I was passionate and had a strong sense of calling. I just knew three years would breeze by. Fast forward a year, and I'm in the middle of taking sixteen credits, working two-part time jobs, and trying to spend time with my wife and kids. I learned that we had more breaking points than we knew of. I reached most of them. One night, with assignments pending, I threw up my hands in frustration. I thought about quitting my studies and finding a

> "I threw up my hands in frustration. I thought about quitting my studies and finding a regular job somewhere."

regular job somewhere.

I expected things to go smoothly. I had made the right decision, so the least I could expect was a neat and tidy experience, right? I slowly learned that just because you decide to do the right thing doesn't mean that doing the right thing will be easy. I should have been disappointed in myself for expecting something that God never promised.

> "Just because you decide to do the right thing doesn't mean that doing the right thing will be easy."

The story of Elijah and the prophets of Baal is considered one of the greatest showdowns in the Bible. The challenge was simple: get the deity that you serve to respond by fire. After an impressive performance that resulted in nothing, the prophets of Baal were exhausted and bloody. Elijah asked for water to be poured over his sacrifice several times before he prayed. Elijah prayed and God responded with fire. You would think that this supernatural sign would be all that Elijah would need to keep his confidence going for years.

It wasn't. Queen Jezebel threatened Elijah's life, and he ran away. The prophet who had dreamed about the possibility of his people returning to God was now afraid for his life. Maybe he thought that once God answered by fire, all opposition would be taken care of and the hard part would be over.

Taking rest in a cave after eating a meal prepared by angels, Elijah seemed to be depressed. Should he have just given up on his new dream for a Israel that would trust God again? Calling down the fire from heaven was the easy part. Trusting God to walk with him when all he had was a dream? That was difficult. When God showed up to Elijah at the cave, Elijah complained that he was the only one left and he was afraid his day were numbered.

Without Eljiah's willingness to face difficulty, two kings might not have received their anointing. As long as Elijah hid in the cave, his replacement would never get the mantle. Elijah needed to stand strong in the hard times so that 7,000 others he had never met could be inspired to keep going too. Elijah's story is a reminder that just because you receive the assurance that God is guiding you doesn't mean that the journey will be easy.

> "Just because you receive the assurance that God is guiding you doesn't mean that the journey will be easy."

"Now Ahab told Jezebel all that Elijah had done, and how he had killed all the prophets with the sword. Then Jezebel sent a messenger to Elijah, saying, "So may the gods do to me and even more, if I do not make your life as the life of one of them by tomorrow about this time." And he was afraid and arose and ran for his life and came to Beersheba, which belongs to Judah, and left his servant there."

I Kings 19:1-3

Reflections:

Based on today's reading, what area(s) of your life might God be calling you to imagine, dream, or plan again?

Day 16

The New Vision May Be Beyond You

Manute Bol is an NBA legend.

Listed at 7'7" tall, Bol was one of the tallest men to ever play the game. Bol's focus in life was twofold, to play the game that he loved and to help was many people from his homeland as he could. A native of Sudan, Bol grew up amid political tensions, and basketball provided a way to experience a better life. It wasn't an easy path to the National Basketball Association, but Bol made it. Noted as a good shot-blocker, Bol still struggled during his NBA career. His career was lackluster, but his journey to the NBA and the hope he gave his country can never be forgotten. Bol died in 2010, but he leaves behind a legacy and a good name.

You've probably never heard of Bol Bol.

Bol Bol is the son of the late Manute Bol. Bol Bol is listed as a top-five basketball recruit who will mostly likely have his pick of colleges. Bol Bol's height (6'10" and probably still growing) and skills have basketball scouts categorizing him as a game changer. From the look of things, Bol Bol has the potential to easily eclipse his father's NBA career and bring even greater honor to Sudan. What if he left as part of his will a ban against his son playing basketball? What if he decided that basketball was a vision that he alone would experience?

David really wanted to build the temple. He had a new vision for worship gatherings. For David, the tent-style sanctuary given to Moses wasn't good enough. He was irritated by the comparison that he lived in a nice palace but the place for God was nothing more than a glorified tent (2 Samuel 7:2). Out of all his military and civil accomplishments, David wanted to list the construction of the temple as his greatest act. Building the temple was on David's bucket list. He probably had plans to have it etched on his tombstone that he built a temple for God. But this was not God's plan. The honor that could have been David's was passed to his son Solomon, the future king.

The temple was David's vision, but the vision would be beyond him. It was at this point that David had a choice. He could either allow his disappointment to frustrate him for the rest of his days or he could set his son up for success. David chose the latter. For the rest of his days, David focused on gathering all materials that Solomon would need to finish the temple. David became the principal financier of a vision that he wouldn't see come to reality.

Just because the new vision starts with you doesn't mean that it always ends with you. God might just drop the new vision in your lap with the intent that you support the person who he has called to carry it out after you.

> "The temple was David's vision, but the vision would be beyond him."

> "Just because the new vision starts with you doesn't mean that it always ends with you."

"Then King David said to the entire assembly, "My son Solomon, whom alone God has chosen, is still young and inexperienced and the work is great; for the temple is not for man, but for the Lord God. Now with all my ability I have provided for the house of my God the gold for the things of gold, and the silver for the things of silver, and the bronze for the things of bronze, the iron for the things of iron, and wood for the things of wood, onyx stones and inlaid stones, stones of antimony and stones of various colors, and all kinds of precious stones and alabaster in abundance. Moreover, in my delight in the house of my God, the treasure I have of gold and silver, I give to the house of my God, over and above all that I have already provided for the holy temple."

I Chronicles 29:1-3

Reflections:

Based on today's reading, what area(s) of your life might God be calling you to imagine, dream, or plan again?

Day 17

What if Giants Could be Defeated?

Buster Douglas took down a giant.

In the late '80s and early '90s, Mike Tyson epitomized boxing greatness. His power and skill in the boxing ring were unmatched by his opponents'. The New York-born Tyson was the undisputed heavyweight champion of the world and even had a video game made about him. He was heralded by many as the champion who might not ever lose. When the schedule showed that Tyson's fight in 1990 was against Buster Douglas, Tyson was the overwhelming favorite. In fact, some considered this a tune-up fight for Tyson. Not to mention the fact that Buster Douglas just didn't look like a champion. This was supposed to be easy pickings for Tyson.

Buster Douglas knocked out Mike Tyson with a shot heard around the world. Tyson had knocked Douglas down in the eighth round, but Douglas had recovered. In the tenth round, Tyson was knocked to the mat for the first time in his career. It was also the first time in his career he was counted out. That day Douglas won a victory for the underdogs. Just over 20 days earlier, Douglas had lost his mother. It was this experience that many say fueled Douglas. Some reports suggest that Douglas make a promise to his mother that he would beat Tyson. Long before the fight, Douglas had a new vision for Tyson's record. The new record would include one loss.

There was no way that David was going to win, right?

Goliath was a champion. David was a shepherd. Goliath killed people for a living. David didn't. Goliath was a battle-tested soldier. David wasn't. Goliath looked like a winner, and David didn't. Goliath should have lived and David should have died, but that's not how the story goes. For 40 days, Goliath taunted the Israelite army. For 40 days, the soldiers of Israel ran away each time Goliath hurled insults at them.

Then David showed up with a new vision for battle. He imagined what could happen if someone were to challenge Goliath. His brothers were irritated at his presence and suggestions. King Saul thought he was sending young David to his death. But David approached Goliath with God-sized confidence. One sling and one rock later, Goliath was dead and David was victorious. In everyone else's mind, there were no options. In David's mind there was only one option, imagining life without the fear of Goliath and the Philistine army.

> "David approached Goliath with God-sized confidence."

Be careful of telling yourself that you're not supposed to win, achieve, or overcome. That's fear talking. Try David's tactic. Imagine what life would like look for you if the giants that you're afraid come tumbling down.

> "Be careful of telling yourself that you're not supposed to win, achieve, or overcome."

"Then David said to the Philistine, 'You come to me with a sword, a spear, and a javelin, but I come to you in the name of the Lord of hosts, the God of the armies of Israel, whom you have taunted. This day the Lord will deliver you up into my hands, and I will strike you down and remove your head from you. And I will give the dead bodies of the army of the Philistines this day to the birds of the sky and the wild beasts of the earth, that all the earth may know that there is a God in Israel, and that all this assembly may know that the Lord does not deliver by sword or by spear; for the battle is the Lord's and He will give you into our hands.'"

I Samuel 17:45-47

Reflections:

Based on today's reading, what area(s) of your life might God be calling you to imagine, dream, or plan again?

Day 18

What Will You Leave Behind?

Each time I look in my garage, I wish I had left more stuff behind.

When I started writing this book, it had been four months since our family moved from Kentucky to Maryland. "Moving," to some people, fits in the category of curse words. The process of moving can challenge everything you have physically, emotionally, and spiritually, even if you have movers!

My wife and I strongly debated about what to leave behind and what to take with us. Our discussions would swing between two extremes. In one conversation we were taking everything. In another conversation we weren't taking anything. Apparently we reached a compromise somewhere along the way. We were both frustrated, boxing up things we hadn't used in months or even years. We finally traveled in a stuffed van across the country. Our "essentials" competed with our ability to ride comfortably to our new home. Today we still struggle to find a place to put many of the things that we couldn't bear to part with.

> "We still struggle to find a place to put many of the things that we couldn't bear to part with."

During the time of Jesus, there were three primary ways in which people received a message from God. Either an angel would show up (this was rare), you would hear it from a priest at the temple, or you would hear it from the teachers in the synagogue. Jesus had a new vision for sharing messages from God. He planned to take the twelve students he was training, equip them for ministry, and then send them out to share what they had been given. Luke's gospel outlines the clear instructions Jesus gave his disciples about packing for the trip. Nothing extra was allowed.

It makes sense when you think about it. The more stuff you travel with, the more stuff you need to keep track of. At every stop on the trip from Kentucky to Maryland, I always had to double-check to make sure my laptop bag was in view. The thought of accidentally leaving it behind troubled me. Imagine the disciples at every stop having to worry about where they put their money, walking stick, or extra food. The time and energy spent keep track of their personal inventory would have taken away from the time and energy they needed to share the gospel.

To be honest, several of the things we brought from Kentucky are just in the way. They are not adding value. I'm committed to them only because I purchased them, not because they help. Now the time and energy it takes to sort and discard will take away from something else I could be doing.

Your new vision may require both some housecleaning and for you to pack lighter for the trip. There are some people, places, and things that will get in the way of the new vision God has for you. Don't force them into a sack and try to carry them anyway.

> "Your new vision may require both some housecleaning and for you to pack lighter for the trip."

"And He called the twelve together, and gave them power and authority over all the demons and to heal diseases. And He sent them out to proclaim the kingdom of God and to perform healing. And He said to them, "Take nothing for your journey, neither a staff, nor a bag, nor bread, nor money; and do not even have two tunics apiece. Whatever house you enter, stay there until you leave that city. And as for those who do not receive you, as you go out from that city, shake the dust off your feet as a testimony against them." Departing, they began going throughout the villages, preaching the gospel and healing everywhere."

Luke 9:1-6

Reflections:

Based on today's reading, what area(s) of your life might God be calling you to imagine, dream, or plan again?

Day 19

A New Vision Demands a New Space

I used to watch a show called Shark Tank.

On the show, people would pitch business ideas to a panel of millionaire investors who had seen amazing success in business. The goal of those pitching ideas was to walk away with at least one investor who decided to partner with them. Those who were able to persuade investors to join them were usually in for the time of their lives.

The stories on Shark Tank that appealed to me the most were the ones in which a family had invented something in their basement or garage, and through working with the investor, the demand for their product increased exponentially. They quickly outgrew the basement or garage and set out to find a new space to run their business. At the beginning their vision was to create another revenue stream for the family. After working with the investor, they started dreaming new dreams. Those new dreams would never have been possible if the family refused to leave the basement or the garage.

> "At nearly every turn, they looked for an excuse to give up on that vision."

The children of Israel were slow to change. Years had passed since God first gave them the vision to go to the Promised Land. At nearly every turn, they looked for an excuse to give up on that vision. Now they were in danger of losing out on the

Promised Land because of something good. For years they had lived near Mount Horeb. Also known as Sinai, this was a place of great significance. This was the place where God came down to talk to the children of Israel and where God gave Moses the Ten Commandments. Horeb symbolized for them the presence of God, and they were content to stay there.

The area was vast, but their thinking was limited. God essentially told them that the new vision He had for the nation was much bigger than the limitations they had placed on their thinking in the desert. God told them to get up from there and go to a new place. I can imagine the leaders debating the reason for leaving. They had food, they had nice tents, they were protected, and to top it all off, they had God on the mountain.

Here's the reality that we are faced with. When God gives new a new vision of the place where He wants you, the place you are in becomes a bad place, even if it's a good place. It was only after moving to the new place that the children of Israel rose to the level of prominence and influence that God had envisioned for them in the first place. Simply put, that new vision that God gives us often requires us to move to a new space. It could be a new space emotionally, a new space socially, or a new space physically, but regardless, it is a new space.

Where might you be in danger of missing out on living up to your God-given potential because you refuse to move to a new space?

> "When God gives new a new vision of the place where He wants you, the place you are in becomes a bad place, even if it's a good place."

"The Lord our God spoke to us at Horeb, saying, 'You have stayed long enough at this mountain. Turn and set your journey, and go to the hill country of the Amorites, and to all their neighbors in the Arabah, in the hill country and in the lowland and in the Negev and by the seacoast, the land of the Canaanites, and Lebanon, as far as the great river, the river Euphrates. See, I have placed the land before you; go in and possess the land which the Lord swore to give to your fathers, to Abraham, to Isaac, and to Jacob, to them and their descendants after them.'"

Deuteronomy 1:6-8

Reflections:

Based on today's reading, what area(s) of your life might God be calling you to imagine, dream, or plan again?

Day 20

New Vision Always Challenges the Culture

I was walking across the parking lot one day toward the Wal-Mart entrance.

Three guys approached me and asked if they could borrow my phone because someone needed help. From their appearance, they looked to be … on second thought, I won't tell you what I assumed their ethnic background to be. Thoughts quickly ran through my head. Is this a trick? Am I about to be robbed? I was always told not to trust people like this.

Reluctantly I handed over my phone. Better for them to take my phone that to beat me up and take my phone, right? A man standing a few feet away shouted to me that what I did was a dumb idea. Moments before approaching me, they had asked him. One of the guys punched in a few numbers and began to describe the situation. The other two begin walking in the other direction. I followed them between two cars. Just ahead of them, I saw a lady lying on the ground. Apparently she had fallen, and they guys were just trying to get her some assistance. They tried to help her themselves but she refused. Maybe she thought they were shady like I did.

Several moments later an ambulance responded to the call, and the lady was taken to the hospital. By this time the three guys had left, and the lady was thanking me for helping her. Little did she know, my cultural bias almost kept her from getting the help that she needed. From that day forward, I refused to look at individuals from that particular group as anything less than what they were, humans, just like me.

The Jewish perspective during the time of Jesus toward other cultures was not the best. They considered anyone who was not of Jewish descent to be cursed. The Jews were the chosen people, and any other race could never measure up. Inferior, barbaric, less than — these would have been the words that came of the mind of a Jewish man who encountered someone from another culture.

> "From that day forward, I refused to look at individuals from that particular group as anything less than what they were, humans, just like me."

During his ministry Jesus challenged the assertions of Jewish culture. He offered salvation to a Samaritan woman. He healed a Roman soldier's servant. He brought life to the daughter of a Canaanite women. All of these people would have fit into the category of inferior. Though Jesus' disciples were present in many of his encounters with people from different backgrounds, they still wrestled with this notion.

Peter's vision on a rooftop fits into this narrative. God was stretching Peter's notion of ministry. He was calling for Peter to revision what sharing the Gospel actually looked like. The picture that Peter received was not the development of a new diet for Jews. Instead, God was asking Peter to bypass cultural biases and be willing to share the message of God with those previously deemed unclean. Eventually this would create tension in Peter's personal life. As long as no other Jews were involved, Peter was okay with this new perspective on ministry.

However, in the presence of others, Peter reverted back to his cultural bias. Eventually Paul would challenge Peter for his flip-flopping.

God's new vision for you may compel you to connect with and minister to those whom society deems less-than. How willing are you to lose social standing or popularity points when God's vision for the next stage of your life calls you to live counter to the popular culture?

> "On the next day, as they were on their way and approaching the city, Peter went up on the housetop about the sixth hour to pray. But he became hungry and was desiring to eat; but while they were making preparations, he fell into a trance; and he saw the sky opened up, and an object like a great sheet coming down, lowered by four corners to the ground, and there were in it all kinds of four-footed animals and crawling creatures of the earth and birds of the air. A voice came to him, "Get up, Peter, kill and eat!" But Peter said, "By no means, Lord, for I have never eaten anything unholy and unclean." Again a voice came to him a second time, "What God has cleansed, no longer consider unholy. "This happened three times, and immediately the object was taken up into the sky."
>
> Acts 10:9-16

Reflections:

Based on today's reading, what area(s) of your life might God be calling you to imagine, dream, or plan again?

Day 21

When God Revisions

I was a bit jealous when one of my best friends purchased an iPod. For years we had carried around those bulky CD wallets with hundreds of our favorite CDs. Now he had the ability to walk around with hundreds of songs in his pocket, and I still had to carry around my bulky wallet. I was intrigued by the technology and badly wanted one for myself. It would be two years before I purchased one for myself, and I struggled to find the words to properly explain how I felt when I transferred my music from CDs to my iPod.

For a few years, the design of the iPod remained roughly the same. Then something amazing was unveiled in 2007. That year the iPod had been revisioned. Instead of a buttons, a wheel, and a screen, the new iPod featured one button and a large screen. It was the iPod touch, and it was a game-changer. I wonder what it would have been like to be in the room during the brainstorming session. Pictures of the development of the iPod over the years might have donned the wall with someone asking the question of what to do next. Then came the idea. Why don't we make a touch-screen version? Today we can hardly imagine what life would be like without our touch-screen devices. It probably all started because a company was willing to revision what was already working.

> "It probably all started because a company was willing to revision what was already working."

The Genesis narrative gives us an account of the creation of Earth. During John's vision on Patmos Island, he gets a glimpse of one of God's revisions. John sees a picture of Earth, version two. It has been reimagined. It has been done over. It has been revisioned. John writes that the first Earth has been scrapped. Despite all the amazing and tragic things that have happened on Earth, John notes that it gets a replacement. Earth is upgraded, totally reinvented from a pile of ashes.

It is hard for us to attempt to dive inside the mind of God. There is a huge chasm between our thoughts and ways and God's. Things that confound and disturb us are no challenge for him. God doesn't stay awake at night scratching his head thinking about what He's going to do. We don't know exactly when God thought about it, but he planned for a new Earth a long time ago. I'm looking forward to the experience.

Several years ago I found my old iPod. It felt clunky and it was awkward to use. I couldn't imagine going back to using it. I'm glad it was revisioned. I wonder if on the new Earth we'll be able to look at pictures or a vision of what the old Earth looked like. Maybe it will look clunky. Maybe it will be awkward to describe. Maybe it will be hard to imagine the idea of going back to that place. No matter what the experience is, I'm sure everyone will be happy that God planned a new one.

It has been reimagined.
It has been done over.
It has been Re:Visioned.

"Then I saw a new heaven and a new earth; for the first heaven and the first earth passed away, and there is no longer any sea. And I saw the holy city, new Jerusalem, coming down out of heaven from God, made ready as a bride adorned for her husband. And I heard a loud voice from the throne, saying, "Behold, the tabernacle of God is among men, and He will dwell among them, and they shall be His people, and God Himself will be among them, and He will wipe away every tear from their eyes; and there will no longer be any death; there will no longer be any mourning, or crying, or pain; the first things have passed away." And He who sits on the throne said, 'Behold, I am making all things new." And He said, "Write, for these words are faithful and true."'

Revelation 21:1-5

Reflections:

Based on today's reading, what area(s) of your life might God be calling you to imagine, dream, or plan again?

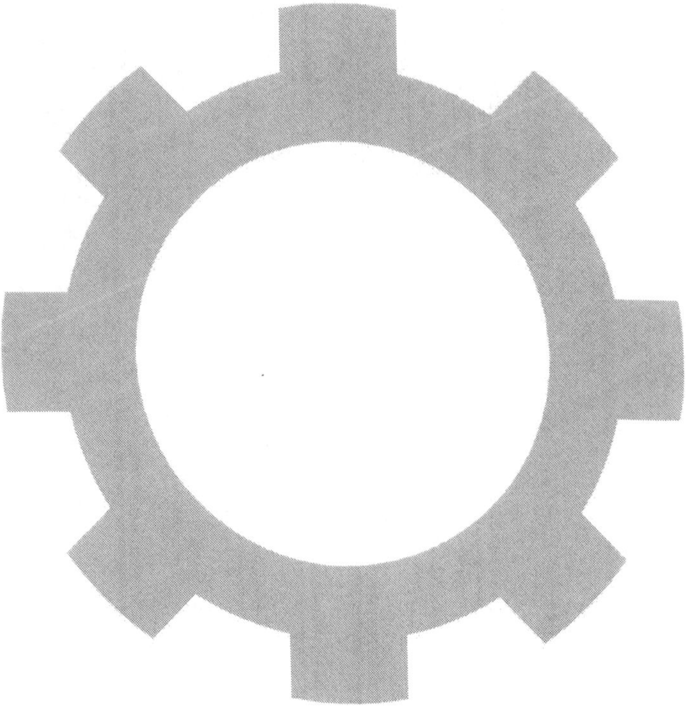

Dear Reader,

At the time of writing this book, I am serving as the lead pastor of a church that is roughly 40 years old. This church has a great history, compelling stories, and clear examples of how God has moved in its past. However, I know that God wants to do some amazing things in our present and future.

The idea for this devotional was originally part of a sermon series entitled *Re:Vision*. The series focuses on much of what you've read already. It wrestles with the question of how we honor what God has done in our past while embracing what he wants to do next in our lives. After a few conversations with close friends, it became clear that more than just those connected with my church needed to hear that God wants them to imagine, dream, and plan again.

Now that you've come to the end of this 21-day journey, my prayer for you is that you take what God has called you to imagine, dream, or plan again and ask for the strength to go forward with that new vision. It won't be easy, and not everyone will understand. But as the pages of scripture continue to reveal to us, those who embrace God's revision will never be disappointed in the end.

Blessings,

Pierre
pierre@pierecquinn.com

"But just as it is written, 'Things which eye has not seen and ear has not heard, and *which* have not entered the heart of man, all that God has prepared for those who love Him.'"

I Corinthians 2:9